Sleepwalker's Guide to Grieving

poems by

Shellie Harwood

Finishing Line Press
Georgetown, Kentucky

Sleepwalker's Guide to Grieving

*Nobody is sleeping in the sky. Nobody, nobody.
Nobody is sleeping...
Let there be a landscape of open eyes
And bitter wounds on fire.
—Federico Garcia Lorca
from "City That Does Not Sleep"*

Copyright © 2023 by Shellie Harwood
ISBN 979-8-88838-220-2 First Edition
All rights reserved under International and Pan-American Copyright Conventions.
No part of this book may be reproduced in any manner whatsoever without written permission from the publisher, except in the case of brief quotations embodied in critical articles and reviews.

ACKNOWLEDGMENTS

The poem "(why I did not) Sleep in the Plagued Years" was published by the *Connecticut Poetry Society*, and received Honorable Mention for the Vivian Shipley Award.
The poem "Photograph of Two Sisters, Memphis, 1902" was first published in the *Tulip Tree Review*, Disruptors Issue.
The poem "Afterswarm," winner of the Nutmeg Poetry Award, 2022, was first published by the *Connecticut Poetry Society*.
The poem "Lost in Sweet Aleppo" was first published in *Connecticut River Review*, 2022.
The poem "What Bloomed in Dresden," second place, Connecticut Poetry Award, was first published by the *Connecticut Poetry Society*.

To the many friends who support me.

And to my husband, Allen, who forever offers me refuge.

Publisher: Leah Huete de Maines
Editor: Christen Kincaid
Cover Art: Somnambule, Paris, Shellie Harwood
Author Photo: Allen Grunerud
Cover Design: Elizabeth Maines McCleavy

Order online: www.finishinglinepress.com
also available on amazon.com

Author inquiries and mail orders:
Finishing Line Press
PO Box 1626
Georgetown, Kentucky 40324
USA

Table of Contents

Sleepwalker's Guide to Grieving 1
Sparrows 2
Afterswarm 3
Zebras 4
White Tulips 5
Lamb is Burning 6
Chrysalis 7
Memorial Days 8
Coda 9
Lessons from My Absent father 10
Burnt Planet 13
Sharp Things 14
Something Small 15
The Complexity of Light 16
At the No Más Gallery 17
Heading for Home 18
Crossing the Rio Grande 19
Passage 20
All Will Break Apart 21
Lost in Sweet Aleppo 22
Photograph of Two Sisters, Memphis, 1902 23
the gosling 24
Death of Another Season 25
Mist Over Cairo 26
What We Take When We Leave 27
Break and End of Days 28
One Hour, Ten 29
The Poet's Widower 30
Two Children Shot Dead in Richmond 31
What Bloomed in Dresden 32
(why I did not) Sleep in the Plagued Years 33
At the Bassin de la Villette, Feb. 2018 34

Sleepwalker's Guide to Grieving

You are naked in the garden, eyes glassed,
digging on hands and knees
in a shaft of moonlight.

I read in The Sleepwalker's Guide to Grief:
never wake them abruptly while in the throes of unearthing,
the heart may erupt,
violence may ensue.

I swing above you in the hanging
egg chair,
watch you clawing the soil.

By dawn
you have uprooted every mud cloaked bulb,
crushed every creped ranunculus,
razed the Stairway to Heaven bearded iris,
and strangled the trumpet lily
known as African Queen.

You have fallen face first into full-on slumber now,
mouth caked with loss, fists full of sod and severed shoots.

I could bring you a quilt from the hall,
or offer you the merciful numbing of frost.
What would it matter?
Regret will pry your eyes wide soon enough,
when the sun begins her baking.

For now,
I cover you loosely, my friend,
in the misplaced dirt from your beloved garden,
up to the tip of your chin,
leave you breathing out and breathing in
only lost things.

Sparrows
    —*for my mother, Lucky*

I take my mother,
the old one, the parchment one, the ashed one,

not the firm assed, high breasted, stiletto prancing one,
but the crumbs of her, to sustain the sparrows and the dusky Dunnock.

Take her in a beaded bag to Paris,
into Père Lachaise, tuck her in beside her dear Piaf,

empty her in, as it were, the fine dust of her,
settle her in, mingle her with the dust of Edith

and the daughter, Marcelle.
Slip her curling ear in tight against

the mouth of La Môme Piaf,
offering this perpetual vibration, these eternal notes

of *Non, je ne regrette rien*.
Lie down with them, humming,

face against cold stone, wrap my limbs around them,
each of us now, a motherless child.

Afterswarm

The day your father died, face down in his hives,
you arrived on my front porch, reeking of honeyed smoke,

your truck bed full of shattered, scarred frames,
hands deep in charred pockets. Said my name.

When he saw the flames he'd called you, as he seldom did,
his only son, but you were too late to stop

the slaughter. Twenty years and twenty hives, torched
and tossed into the stagnant pond.

Six hundred thousand bees felled by a stranger's matches,
too much time too free on cruel hands, colonies kicked and hurled,

toppled while they slept by the rage of unknowns. Your father's
flashlight shook in his hand as the dazed survivors swarmed it,

stinging the only hands they loved or knew. Your father threw back
his head, you said, howled like a torn beast for his incinerated queens.

And as you sprayed the firestorm, he fell to his knees and broke to see
the floating brood frame in the pond, stunned bees still caring for the brood.

The night your father died, having flown through this life on the
vibrating backs of his bees, humming along with them as he

could not with you, that night we sat in the cab of the old pickup,
my face turned down and away, while you wept for the man

who roughed you with his honeyed hands, and was late to loving you.
Wept, too, for the queenless swarm and the fallen queens.

Zebras

It was the summer
a zeal of zebras broke from the farm in Maryland,
thundered free like thoroughbreds on the stretch.
Three together, two in a pair, at the curve,
knowing they had to split up to survive,
cheered by us as they raced for the suburban savanna.

It was the summer
they pulled out the alligator
down in Mississippi, on the Louisiana line.
Sliced him open, 13 feet, 750 pounds,
the past pouring out of him:
a plummet, pear-shaped, from 1700,
plank of cypress, 18 inches long.
Bones, hair, flesh and feathers,
a broken arrowhead.
Solitary bullet, never fired.
Stomach contents of a thousand and a thousand years.
Floating time capsule, nothing now but a hunter's prize.

A volcano bled out over the Canary Islands that summer,
like a dragon's tongue, this plume from LaPalma.
Whole towns smoldered away on the west coast, in Plumas County,
while Haitian refugees in Del Rio gathered like a fallen murmuration
under the international bridge.

I said to someone:
Take me away to the world's edge, far from the host of sorrows.
Let me lie there. Let me dangle feet from the California coast
into aqua water.
But then the oil came spilling out,
plumes of oil now.
And the yellowtails washed up on Huntington, where I lay in the slick,
and pelicans were dipped in ink.
The black tarred cormorants and the asylum of loons lined up beside me, pleading.
I closed my eyes and ears,
thought of the dazzle of zebras madly running,
corralled before they got where they were going.
Turned my heart off,
so weary was I, and so weak from the knowing.

White Tulips
—for Jack, on his suicide

As if the blast that took you
did not enter through your mouth,
exit through a black hole in the ceiling,
lifting the shingles you so carefully laid.

As if the calico slept on in unshaken patchwork
on the windowsill, alongside the tulips
bending like white swans from their vase, unquivering.

As if I could travel from it, I rush headlong through borders.
I bare my chest in India, wild and unforgiving,
throw my head back, open wide
my mouth to the blood rain in Kerala;
singe my knees, my elbows in the Philippines,
in the Palina,
to crawl through the smoke bath of the bonfire,
shed spirits of the dead.

Look what cannot be undone, in the rearrangement. Can you not see it?
Look what prevails, what will not splatter:

White tulips in the window
arching above the cut glass,
survive somehow
the   spattering,
    stunned by their own sudden
        red   and pulsing variegation.

Lamb is Burning

I remember I did call before we came. I did say
are we still on for dinner? You could have told me:
Something's come up, the west coast is blazing,

the power is gone, I'm under the weather,
he is not right within himself, send the extraction team.
But you said, *I'm cooking lamb.*

I asked what wine would pair with sacrifice,
and you made a strangled sound deep in your
throat, something like laughter. And so we came.

Your sleeves were long, buttoned tight to your wrists,
in August. You boiled potatoes with your sunglasses on.
The oven crackled. *Lamb is burning,* he said.

You flew to pull it out, into the already crackling air,
let it rest. I said low to you, *Please let me help you. Can't
I do something?* You pointed to a scorching sauce,

armed me with a wooden spoon. Nothing to do but stir.
Eyes on you beside me at the cutting board as you julienned
peppers with a paring knife. His hand snaked out to cup your

breast as he passed for another beer. I said to you, *can I talk to you
for a minute?* But you said, *everything will be cold.*
So, we let you lead us to table, to all this bounty,

where we ate your leg of lamb, smothered in mint jelly,
sharp blades of carrots, baby potatoes bruising in butter,
swallowing hard while you ate the hoof.

I couldn't raise you all the day after.
By evening, it was on my screen and in the local paper
and I was knelt at porcelain, savior to no one,

retching your last meal.

Chrysalis

I'm writing today
about the nest of baby cormorants
grey as grief,
red mouths, wide open wounds
rimmed with yellow,
mouths looking more like flowering things.
About finding them and trying to feed them,
with their mother fled, or dead, or losing interest;
about the soil, the sand, the crumbs,
the sallow worms that would not nourish.
I'm pulling the paper nearer to me,
as one does who works from memory,
drawing the image close for inspection, close for the truth of it,
when the cormorants close their mouths
at once, go silent.

And I see my mother
holding my dying sister on her lap.
Her arms hang heavy at sides, my mother's,
not daring touch.
The chair goes on rocking.
She moves her mouth without sound, my mother,
as you would if you held a chrysalis,
coaxing it to open, to become.
And knowing what will soon be lost in darkening,
she keeps her eyes fast on my sister's face,
bidding her to stay while guiding her away
on through the wretched sorrow of this rusting light.

Memorial Days

Something's always coming for us,
some pain we'd neglected to rehearse for.
Along the southern border
toddlers tossed over the fence now
like crumpled paper, like empty wrappers in slow wind.
Nine and a quarter minutes of a knee to throat
on a lazy Monday in the deep of Minnesota May.
A neon towel unfurled across Sumatra sands
before the black wall of tsunami closes in.
And in the farmer's teeming marketplace,
someone's son cradles a weapon of war,
spraying the tomatoes from the vines,
babies from the breasts of mothers.
Scattering blood and berries wild in the gravel.
Slicing open the melons
and the fragile peace of a Saturday.

If something is coming for us,
fangs out, jaws wide open,
lock the flags at half-mast,
then make love to me once more against the wall
in the backstairs hall. We'll fall together, unlikely soldiers that we are,
onto the Persian runner, struggling for breath,
for fleeting joy we've known.
If something is always coming,
let me circle and circle back to you
like an old dog chasing sleep.
When they break the door down, arms drawn high,
I want my terror pressed up tight
against your own.

Coda
    —for s.e.

first kiss, yours
at thirteen, in hot rain
lying stained in wet grass
from the yard that embraced the house
you would leave
then come home to die in

your sweet mother
viewed years later through the window
hair undone
stood sentinel behind the piano bench
begging you to play on
through the cancer
her hands resting on your shrinking shoulders
fingers miming your last notes
her lips sealed in a bitter line

her lips, much as they were
all the decades back
pursed through curtain lace
watching as your fingers played
across my new breasts
our mouths fused and bruising

you breathing life to me
and while I could, me into you

Lessons from My Absent Father

I.

I was always told, whenever I asked, that one of two things
happened to my phantom father:

either he hitched away, burning across the sky
on the tail of a comet, or he stole my grandmother's

'51 Chevy and burned across every highway on the map
on his way from Idaho to the furthest tip of northern

Michigan, where someone new was waiting, stopping
only when he skidded on November ice into a

frozen lake somewhere in the Dakotas, settling the
frame of the now forever rusting Chevy deep

in the lakebed, where no divers could be paid to go, and
too deep to ever come home from, even after a thaw.

I read about the comets when I was younger,
so I knew they were cosmic snowballs

of gases and dusty particles that orbit the sun.
A frozen comet is the size of a small town, any

town, like mine, that wasn't a city yet, but dreamed
of someday being a city. And when the orbit

brings this comet close to the sun, it heats and chews
and spews its gases into a glowing head bigger

than all the planets, and it grows a tail to switch when
it's restless, and it's all about the volatile ices showing off

for earth while keeping distance from the sun.
I think my father didn't fall through a lake on his way

to disappearing. He just knew how to streak away through
the heavens, staying faint and unspectacular, while arcing

sixty moons across the sky.

II.

my father taught me by vanishing
how to be unseen
when the time came
how to hide in the tall grass

how to slip thin and threadbare as paper
through the screen door
easing it back to the jamb
    nothing to rattle in the pockets
    not coins nor knife
    nor metal mirror for reflection
shoes in hand

taught me
to drop to my belly
in the tall grass
face to dirt   untwitching
one with the inchworms
stock-still while winds passed over
drowning my name
even as they called for me

and about that moment
    only one
where I could choose whether
to rise up
face the wind and howling voices
and heave for home
or pull myself by roots
like a deserting soldier through the mire
and vanish into the marshes

disappearing is the easy part
but only the hummingbird and the dragonfly
know the art of reverse flight
    even my father
had no lesson for this

III.

how can I explain my rage
when in mid-life lost
in a New York taxi
      the city's chaos
        reflected in rain-lacquered lanes
I saw through the weeping window
a man
bend
without umbrella
to tie a small girl's shoe

lingering low like that
long after the lacing

crouched dripping face to face
long after the light had changed

Burnt Planet
—for Morgan and Nicholas

Our babies did not know the planet was burning.
They woke star-eyed and sticky-fingered,
fat fists filled with dappled daylight,
mouths open for the first worms
and mama's fresh cream warm from breast to belly.
They did not know to care for icecaps melting.
They woke stuffed into sausage snowsuits,
thrown into fresh powdered winter,
tipping top heavy into drifts,
lifting puffy arms to fly with magpies,
starlings, and the Northern flickers.

Our babies did not turn nor toss in lost sleep
for the ghosting snow leopard, the golden bamboo lemur.
Their mouths moved and sucked in dreams,
throats never dry, tides never high;
grew, sleep-taught,
learning the names of every living thing, every starfish
that awaited them.

Our babies, mine and yours, chased wind,
lived on fierce love and wonder,
sailed on trumpeter swans.
They did not know the blood on snow, sequoias burning.
What they had not yet loved was not yet lost to them—
the coral, the mapping dance of bees,
the serenity of wild beasts,
the unburnt star.

Sharp Things

In the house that raised me,
where I did cower sometimes
from the words and objects, the sharp things
launched by fury,
I held still as shadow
sometimes,
leaning in to learn the
language of the harsh mouth;
the desperate,
the shattered syntax.

To learn the sounds
of the poultice, hot and moist
wrapping around the injury.

From that house,
a linguist of that love,
I poured myself out, melted
into your cup
and down your throat, like sweet cream,
soothing and soundless.
And sometimes, too,
stepped out, a glinting blur of blades.
Too sharp, too sharp to ever hold.

Something Small

Have you stood, hands shaking in Kraków, fingers knotted
like the roots of rutabagas
spread out across the carved credenza?
Tracing the patterns etched by your grandfather's hand
into the heartwood,
trembling along the beveled edge,
as someone—a child you love, a niece, a neighbor—
whispers quick and low,
No, not that. No. Too big. They're coming now.
Only something you can take with hands.
Take something small.

Have you stopped to caress the cabriole
curving out from the seat of the brocade chair
like a ballet dancer's limb leaps through the air ahead of the other?
And thought of Ima. Who waited in this chair to meet
the man who would be your father.
But the voice, again: *They're coming! Take only something small!*
Have you reached then for a brooch, a hatpin,
or a peacock patterned cup,
recalling in that instant that you wear the dress today, the damned and only one
with the absence of pockets?
And nothing now but the pounding of boots.
Nothing for carrying.

Or maybe you have stood by Tijuana waters and
lifted your child who stares with her great eyes,
into the sagging boat, into the panga,
whispered across the hull, *No puedo venir.*
I cannot come.
Shouted, *Take her over! There is room there. Por favor.*
Make room to save her.
Algo pequeño....

Maybe you are learning it now,
where you are standing.
The sagging weight of carrying,
of saving something small.

The Complexity of Light

All I know of the complexity of light
I learned as a child
watching my mother in morning,
legs curled under her,
black coffee in the white mug,
arm trailing the back of the fading
green sofa, eyes facing away out the window,
traveling from me.
The tricks it would play
across her profile, shadows
re-carving her cheekbones,
casting the corner of her mouth
first up, then down.

And in the evening
the uncertain slant of it, as sun abandoned,
flickering her long and dark hair from auburn
to black,
bangs cut sharp to the arched brows,
the heavy veil of her eyelids,
looking in the red shift
like my Cleopatra,
one hand reaching for the asp,
the other, always, for retreating light.

At the No Más Gallery

Just over the border here, they carve
out the immigrant wombs, display them

pickled in apothecary jars. They float and
gape like hungry mouths, forever empty now.

There are other curiosities, of course, for
your amusement: lips sealed shut, bobbing in

fish bowls, asking for nothing; a vast array
of hearts cleaved open, chambers still bloated

with sand and hungry secrets. But mostly, the No Más
Gallery is all about the pear-shaped uteruses suspended

in the pickling jars. For twenty dollars, there is a man
in a doctor's coat, who'll guide the tour, in English only.

He gestures like a grand ringmaster all around the gallery.
Come close, he tells you. *Look at these beauties.*

And should the bile rise in your throat, he'll quickly
assure you: *Oh, they can't hurt you. They carry*

nothing new to rob you blind in alleyways.
They carry nothing at all.

No, no. No tears at the No Más.
The wombs are free from carrying.

It's very clear to me now, he'll tell you, why
they were so desperate to cross over here.

Heading for Home

On your dying day
we met at your paddock
to feed apples to your Appaloosa,
leaning against the slats
to watch her amble the fence,
stopping to bite the tart fruit,
to nuzzle your face, fill up on the familiar smell of you.

We didn't know, not yet, that this
was your dying day,
only that you clung to the fencepost for balance,
your face collapsing in on itself,
your chest concave,
your mane of mahogany hair,
once thick between my fingers,
tufted now, and nearly gone.

Back in the old neighborhood
you were the King,
moving through the back alleys,
chest puffed up and outward.
The other boys followed behind you,
pelvises thrusting forward,
their shoes fitting into your dusty footprints
in the roadway,
spitting where you spat,
their fingers curling cool and loose
through belt loops, loose tobacco on their lips,
dancing street backup to you.

Today your fingers shake when you reach to stroke
the Appaloosa.
I remind you that you were King, in the day,
you remind me that I gave it up for you.
We need no string wrapped round our fingers, to remember.
These things we carry in our bones, know to be true.

You thank me for driving out, slip an apple in
my pocket for the long trip home,
press your forehead up against mine,
as you do with the old racehorse when she pauses, as if to pray.
You hang onto her mane, heads together, in my memory.
She makes a sound deep in her throat.
Grief sounds that way.

Crossing the Rio Grande

In the dream I walked for days from Guatemala with dirt in my mouth,
and crossed in darkness over the Rio Grande.
I know it was a dream and not a memory because I have never been forced
to cross a river for freedom with a child on my back, clinging hard
like a baby opossum, and I cannot swim. And we were alive.
Did I mention the child, or the strength of the current at fifty nine feet, at
the deepest part?
Or the place where the river bends and shrinks
and we could walk on water over the border on whatever legs survived.

Did I say that the boy I carried was drenched, but free from drowning?
Did I say he was brave and made no sound?
And because dreams are like this,
I remembered right where I was going, and my feet, barely blistered, knew
their way on the ground.
My old friend Lizabeth opened the door for us, young and fair as I last saw her,
and wrapped the boy in a blanket of gold.
Put his name in her mouth to keep it warm.
Then she dried the silver stranding in my thinning hair.
And salvation should be that easy, shouldn't it?
Someone waiting to cup your wet face in their hands, no matter the dream
you're chasing.
Someone to say, "I would have known you anywhere."

Passage

We would lie together
in the damp grass of our youth
and count the constellations,
trace with fingers in the air
tendrils of hair of Cassiopeia,
the sword of Orion, claws of Ursa Major.
Worship at the Northern Cross.
The old ones gathered by lamps
in the windows of rooms we'd not grown into,
murmuring of Laos and Cambodia,
of rumblings in Selma,
while we cocooned in sleeping bags,
unaware of the rising of earth's sooty smoke,
blackening the wings of Cygnus the Swan
up along the Milky Way.

It was all about the skies back then
when we were seven or ten
in our small town,
hands clasped behind our head,
eyes fixed on the heavens.
Still blessedly untaught
about the otherness of others; untouched by savagery of this planet,
together we scanned the night for proof of Sputnik's solitary passage.
And together, how we christened every newborn star.

All Will Break Apart

In the ambulance, the beast,
as it howled through morning rush,
something dropped from the ceiling

loosened, undone,
dangled as oxygen masks
through storms in turbulence do,

swinging wildly above me
where I lay and did not think once
of plaque breaking within my artery,

the clot forming, blocking blood in its flow.
Did not think of the starving of the heart,
but of all else fragile, things that break apart.

My husband's feet, bare on sharp pavers
as he watched us shriek away, my children's sleep,
far off in other towns, broken open by the ringing.

Broken, like trust, like the spider's web,
bubbles in air, a collapsing tower,
a toppled cone of profiteroles.

Thought of old lace, then, that tears
as muscle does, as my shirt when
they cut it free, as silken stockings do,

of eggshells and sidewalks and chests that crack,
bomb blasted windows that burst,
a thoroughbred's leg on a muddy track.

All things will break apart. All.
All, but especially the heart,
as silence is shattered by the calamitous

awakening of crows, the assault of garbage trucks,
the venomous hiss of sprinklers striking morning lawns,
by sirens cleaving the peace to salvage a life,

to salvage a breath expected, and counted on
for the breaking of just one more
hushed, unpromised dawn.

Lost in Sweet Aleppo

Your mother's body was washed
by you and your sister,
wrapped in four pieces of Damascus linen
for the burial.
Your hands are raw when you return to me.

Your face is a hard stone, eyes dark and dry,
heart clenched in your teeth.
I pool oils in my palm to warm them,
I knead your aching hands.

Tell me about your home, I say to you.
Say what you have lost.
You say your mother is a lamp gone out,
you swallow her name. You speak instead
of the cat man of Aleppo,
who stayed behind to tend the rubble
and the orphan cats when Aleppo fell.
The more he feeds, the more they multiply.
No one returns to claim the ghosts he saves.

You shed tears only for a lone bald ibis called Zenobia,
who has not been told of her own extinction,
and searches all of Syria for one to love.
There is no music now. She knows no song.

For every grain of sand,
there are ten thousand stars, you say to me.
You can see them all from sweet Aleppo,
now that the lights are gone.

Photograph of Two Sisters, Memphis, 1902
    —for Hattie

Shall I show you
the sticky molasses air in Memphis, in August, 1902;
how thick it lay
when the strangers drove in
in a fancy automobile filled to the roof with money
from a gold coast
to buy my grandmother away?

And the supper table
laid out with so very little,
and my grandmother Harriet, at ten, above the boiled beets,
so very plain.
And Eleanor, radiant at five, in her blue skirts,
cheeks bruised sunset pinks from pinching, haloed curls on her head.
Oh, but this is the pretty one.
Do you want her? Harriet's mother said.
Take her instead.

Shall I show the photograph
of Eleanor in sepia, screaming backwards facing in the auto,
hands splayed out on tear- stained glass,
rumbling away?

Shall I explain how
Harriet arranged her dingy skirts around her
lifted her chin and posed,
that Eleanor would remember her sister
from the road like that, waiting?
And the others would see, too,
the beauty behind them, draped on porch stairs,
gasp at the mistake they'd made.

Shall I tell you
that the pain my grandmother swallowed
rearranged itself inside her,
twisting and digging into the marrow,
where it burrowed and breathed
and for eighty-five years ate its fill?

Shall I say what she said
when I asked how long she waited?
Sweet girl, I never left there.
Shall I say she's waiting still.

the gosling
>*—for Uvalde, for Newtown*

I know so much more now
about what can and cannot be saved.

The orphaned gosling, all fuzz, no feather,
cradled in to a chick's old breeder box,

kept from blinding light. Geese need geese,
I know, but in the company of mirrors,

on a heating pad set very low, I kept you
fox-proof and breathing until they came for you.

And my dragon flowers, maimed by frost,
rescued, snouts gaping. Resisting all urges

to clip away the dead leaves, I shrouded them
in black cloth, misted them slowly back,

watched the living tissue survive the freeze.
But what if I opened a door one morning,

let something out that never came back to me?
Kissed it, licked and smoothed its downy hair,

released it to a wild it had no wing for.

I cannot wrestle the clock, bend back its hands.
Breach a door judged just unbreachable.

I curl up beside the unsaved.
My body has not warmth to keep them through the night.

I whisper words like benevolence,
hum to them what has been salvaged,

remind them of the gosling, the frozen dragon flower.
Still, they moan and toss, bereft of sleep.

None of it enough, not nearly,
in this godforsaken gloaming hour

Death of Another Season
-for my father

I am outside a crumbling service station
that glows like a golden lantern
in the desert
doors chained, drained pumps limp
and sleeping.

White moths are lost ghosts
fluttering against florescent bulbs,
the empty promise of neon.

There is a basket, wailing, on cracked concrete,
a baby inside, trapped on its back like a poisoned beetle,
arms and legs clawing to sky.
A man climbs in a white truck,
calls as he goes *I won't be a minute*
and his wheels spin out and burn the dusty road
into clouds of napalm.

By now you've figured out there is no child,
no basket at all, no one returning,
no gas station glowing at the edge of town.

Only me here on the back porch,
up against the wildlife refuge,
my eyes on the white moths
ghosting against a bare bulb,
my ears trained on the chant of tree frogs
drunk and lusting for mates before last call.

Or, knowing their own sorrow,
keening shoulder to shoulder
at the border of the wild,
lamenting the death of yet another season.

Mist Over Cairo

On one of the last nights of this, the cruelest year,
I heard that you danced on a table
in a little place in Cairo.
Heard you danced with your mane swirling
over your face, on the final night of your life,
on the sturdy top of table seven.
Table seven. Where we sat once
in a softer year, raised our glasses
just before the humidity lifted its skirts
and for a moment we could see, in distance,
the pyramids of Giza.
Only that table, the waiter had whispered.
Only from there will you see them rise like three
firm breasts out of the hot sands.
Wait for it there.

We sat alive together that day and drank thick beer
too rich for even the god, Osiris;
watched the pyramids shimmer and sizzle.
And pain was elsewhere
as you lay your face against my beating chest.
Écouter son coeur, you told me. Listen to your heart.
Or maybe it was *corazón* you said, or *cuore*.
You loved in every language.

In ancient times, the heart was weighed by gods
against a feather
to see if it was light enough to travel
with the dead one to the afterlife.
When your heart, alone in a harsh time, dancing,
froze on the top of table seven,
I hope that it was lighter, far, than Egyptian air.
Weightless, free falling.
Nothing, in the end, my friend, but fine mist over Cairo.

What We Take When We Leave

when I left you
I did not leave alone
but took you with me
though you didn't know

took you disassembled
part and parcel   I am sorry for that
tucked as you were
under the contours and the openings of me

first the long threads
of your fingers folded into prayer
your mouth
slightly parted
as if to say   no never leave
or to kiss the nape of neck
apply your pressure to the open wound
of my departure

then your heart   a tiny chamber of it
pulsing hard against the carpet bag
as I stole away without you   and with you within

and you
believing even now
that you are where you are
when all along
you were long gone from where you were
but rather
pieced like broken colored glass
through me

and we are a traveling mosaic
as we move the years

gleaming tiles of your eyes
flecked into mine
your stolen touch   embedded
under secret folds of me

you'll feel the chill of it sometimes there where you think you are
something cooling in you now   still burns in me

Break and End of Days

At the break of day, if you were so lucky,
it was you and the old man
at the border by the stream
casting into calm water, in wait of the rippling.

Your head reeling
from the moment of the fish
pulling out on the light line
from the spinning rod,
the battle and blur in the holding net,
the sweet relief of the release.

And the osprey in mid-air above you,
talons locked in a catch too heavy to carry,
plummeting from sky with treasure, both lost in the saving,
without resurfacing.

At the end of the day there was always
the cicada click, a flick of heat lightning
and the thunder's low growl, like a mad dog's warning;
clouds grown black,
swollen and quickening, and the

long road up ahead
under cadaver skies,
scanning for the funnel, the rain's bomb,
the hurricane's eye.

Just the big man, you on his shoulders now,
arms tightening around his neck,
constricting his only words:
we've stayed too long.

Always his breath, ragged from the weight of you,
up the high hill, hoping heart will hold,
pumping hard
to outrun the darkening.

One Hour, Ten
> *"Grief makes one hour ten."* —Shakespeare, King John

I know a woman who misplaced her child
and never did find him.
A boy of six sent up to time out for his troubles.
Troubles all forgotten now—the foul word, the
tantrum, the heels dug deep in resistance—trivial,
long-gone and wished back now.
A boy sent, loved, for an hour to ponder the
solar system dangling from his ceiling, the bears
and elephants wallpapered to his room, perpetually
tumbling in astronaut suits amidst the sharpest stars,
while he thought, as he'd been told, about what he
had done or not done, and thought about or shouted
out or whatever else he ought not have done that
might have torn a new hole in the universe.
And then was simply gone.
She went up, sorry on her lips, with hot cornbread
in a sea of honey butter, found window open wide,
curtains of moons and planets blowing free,
waving him goodbye.
The boy evaporated. Stolen by aliens, or someone
with a collapsing ladder. Or him somewhere scuffed
and scratched from scuttling the trellis down.
And that was the end of it. He was never found.
And every hour she lives is ten now.
And she walks so carefully these days,
as if stepping out across his bones,
and keeps her eyes off of the stars.

The Poet's Widower

Before,
he would watch her write in her sleep,
words moving under her eyelids
like insects scurrying back and forth,
carving out new worlds in her,
and he would turn away, breath held,
when she rose from the bed to grope
in dark for paper and pen.

Later,
he lay silent witness, afraid to follow
when she tunneled deep under the
floorboards, paced the catacombs
under the old house, under the city,
came home smelling of damp
images, slippers worn through.

Now,
he will keep watch from high windows
for her on occasion, even after the vanishing,
eyes strained for the shape of her in the
yawning street, once catching sight
of her passing beneath the street lamp
home to him from night.
He could never be sure of it.
From a distance, grief moves like any other
shadow, caressing first, then smothering
the light.

Two Children Shot Dead in Richmond

that pain you blink and bury
sleep with in a cavernous bed
your back turned cold against it
that rattles in your throat when breathing

that pain you fuck some nights
eyes seared shut
lamp bulb twisted out and on the floor
that you wire your mouth slit tight to moan for

that you boil with the morning egg
unpeel and squish between sharp teeth
and the bloody tongue
dress like a wound and make presentable
prop onto busses and trains
slip into thigh-highs and tunnels
drag home again
over brittle shoulder
like a drunken cadaver

that pain.
tear it apart piece by quivering piece
feed it to the baying strays
see what they can make of it

What Bloomed in Dresden

When the shriveled men feel need again
to invade another country
and the talk talk talk is tanks rolling in,
missiles launched, air raids, and nuclear options;
when the earth begins again to shudder,
I go to the cupboard and pull down the chipped and yellowed tin
where my people, mostly unknown to me,
left recipes copied in my grandmother's palsied hand,
pick a comfort card, any old card, and begin.

When I hear of refugees and mortar shells, artillery,
I begin to assemble Berniece's applesauce cake,
spiced with my childhood,
and I sift and sift, soak raisins on through the sirens,
while the shelling rocks the counters
five thousand counted miles away from me.
My arm spent from mixing, I pour brown batter
in the cracked glass pan, as all the women who share my blood
have poured it, secure it in its oven, wait for it to bubble and rise.

When I wait, I think of Ukraine, of Afghanistan,
of Vietnam, Iraq, and Normandy.
And I wonder what bloomed before bombs in Dresden,
what flies or crawls or claws its way out of Ukraine.

I ask the internet to show me the national bird
of Ukraine, the color of wings to watch for as it makes its frantic way
under the radar, out of choking skies.
Two birds are pictured, white stork and nightingale.
Which is it, then? I have no one to call in Kyiv to ask,
which creature flies for you?

When I hear that they have breached the border of Chernobyl zone,
when I am breaking from the massacre in Bucha,
I pull Berniece's cake from the oven, hold it hot and close
against me, carry it steaming outside where
there are still wild and hungry things.

I fill my own mouth first, in handfuls sticky with raisins
and soft fruit; crumbs fall like cardamon tears.
The rest, I crumble along the fence line
for the nightingale or the white stork.
Whichever might land here, gasping from invasion,
stumbling its way to me.

(why I did not) Sleep in the Plagued Years

I wanted to wake up stunned by something,
shaken awake by something to wake for.
A bit that was startling,
that bolted me up from the
900 thread count.
A horn I had grown overnight
from my temple.
A new variety of courage blistering my skin,
urging me to run naked into the street
to fight for something I'd squandered,
some tiny shred of freedom I'd neglected to save.

Wanted to wake
to the shock of a strange hand on my breast,
someone's I'd never heard of,
an "oh my god who are you and
how did you know to put your hand
just there, just like that?"

Or wake with a new untranslated voice
gushing out of me,
like those people who suddenly speak in tongues
or play Bach's Concerto in A Minor
without a lesson on the strings.

Wanted to wake and remember
some previous life
I'd lived in Kazakhstan
or Yemen
and begin to rock myself backwards and forward,
wet with relief
for living this one in a country humane where
I will escape artillery.
Unless, of course, someone should burst in, guns ablaze,
while I was sleeping. That would be a careless mistake, I suppose.

I bargain that I will sleep again
only when this world will wake to surprise me
with a simple morning paper
unfolded in my lap,
bleached and blank and horrorless,
newsless and bodyless, silent as an empty shroud.
Something unstained and glorious, something pristine,
something bloodless to wrap the fish for dinner in.

At the Bassin de la Villette, Feb. 2018

It will happen in a heart's single contraction.
One moment,
you will bask in a pool of unexpected February sun,
at the Paname, in Paris,
on the Quai de la Loire,
watching an old man lean in from the dock
to push off a young boy in a slender boat,
whispering his last instructions,
mottled hands and rattling voice, both merciful,
before the boy begins to row.
And you will be taught by this moment, as you shoot it,
be a student of it, alone at the oars,
letting the old man's voice reach out to launch you,
to guide you home.
And the text will come through then
with news from home, news of the Parkland shooting,
of what merciless arms can do.
And you will fold inward, aperture closing, light withdrawn;
losing sight of the boy, of his faithful tutor,
of this peaceable lesson, in this peaceable dawn.

And, oh, what will become of us
when all the basins have run dry
and all the tender hands are gone?

Shellie Harwood is a poet, playwright, actress and teacher with a varied background in writing and theatre. She has taught Acting, Communication, and Poetry/Literature at universities, colleges and theatres in California, Idaho, Utah, Tennessee, and Connecticut. She has an MA in playwrighting, and has written several plays, including *Ember Days, Vicious Union,* and *Another Bite of the Moon*. Shellie has worked as an actress, performing throughout the country in regional and repertory theatres. She was born and raised in Idaho, but has spent much of her life moving about the country with her family. She is married, has one daughter, Morgan, and a son, Nicholas.

Shellie has traveled throughout Europe, and lived and wrote for a year in Paris, France in 2018, where she wrote and explored the city. She now lives in Connecticut with her husband, Allen. "I love the dramatic snowstorms and the spectacular autumns in New England, but still find myself missing Paris. I had a profound "land memory" experience when I first arrived in Paris…as if I had lived there before, as if I was already a part of the place, somehow. And it is, of course, a writer's dream. Gertrude Stein said, 'America is my country, but Paris is my hometown.' I feel that…"

Writing has always been a passion for Shellie. She has written since she was very young, and has performed her work at readings and festivals, but it is only during the recent pandemic that she has begun to compile her poetry and distribute it for publication. Shellie's poems have been published in *Oberon, TulipTree Review, Mudfish 22, Sixfold Poetry Summer 2020, Connecticut River Review* and *Connecticut Literary Anthology*. She received Honorable mention in the Vivian Shipley Poetry Contest, for her poem "(why I did not) Sleep in the Plagued Years," Honorable Mention for "Photograph of Two Sisters, Memphis, 1902" in the *TulipTree* Disruptors issue, and was the 2022 winner of the Nutmeg Poetry Award, for her poem, "Afterswarm". Shellie was a finalist for the 2022 Montreal International Poetry Prize.

Shellie was awarded The Oberon Herbert Poetry Prize, established in honor of the revered Polish poet, Zbigniew Herbert. The award, for 2021, was presented by representatives of the Oberon Project and the Zbigniew Herbert Foundation of Warsaw. This honor and cash award was presented to Ms. Harwood for her poem "With My Sister, in a Tornado Warning," for "displaying what Herbert considered essential: semantic transparency; using words as windows into emotions."

She is currently working on a full-length book of collected poems, *Feast for the Madlings*.

www.ingramcontent.com/pod-product-compliance
Lightning Source LLC
Chambersburg PA
CBHW022125090426
42743CB00008B/1006